AF449755

A Voice for Global Citizens: a UN World Citizens' Initiative
A Report of the Campaign for a UN World Citizens' Initiative

Authored by Dr. James Organ and Dr. Ben Murphy

Published in 2019 by Democracy Without Borders, Democracy International, CIVICUS: World Alliance for Citizen Participation

We wish to thank Global Justice Now for their kind support.

Cover design & layout: Rafael Natal – www.rafaelnatal.com

ISBN 978-3-942282-16-1

Visit our website at
www.worldcitizensinitiative.org

A Voice for Global Citizens:

a UN World Citizens' Initiative

A Report of the Campaign for
a UN World Citizens' Initiative

By Dr. James Organ and Dr. Ben Murphy

Contents

Executive Summary

The present report recommends that the United Nations (UN) should develop its democratic legitimacy through the creation of the instrument of a World Citizens' Initiative (WCI) by which global citizens can place proposals on the agenda of the UN General Assembly or the UN Security Council. This paper makes the case that a WCI is legally feasible and aims to provide the impetus for the discussions that will lead to its establishment.

The paper offers background on the concept of citizens' initiatives and discusses challenges to the formalisation of direct citizens' participation in the environment of the UN. The experience of the European Citizens' Initiative (ECI), a European Union instrument that allows citizens to propose legislation to the European Commission, and lessons to be learned from it are examined. A legal framework for the establishment of a WCI is considered in detail. The report recommends that the instrument of a WCI could be established as a subsidiary organ of the UN, under Article 22 of the UN Charter, if such an instrument was supported by a two-thirds majority of the General Assembly. This would include the adoption of detailed rules of procedures and the creation of a WCI Administrative Board.

According to this report, the functioning of a WCI would follow three steps: (1) Registration, (2) collection of support and (3) submission and response.

The report recommends that each WCI would be registered by an organising committee that consists of individuals who may not hold an official political office and who are not formal representatives of civil society organisations. Further, the WCI organising committee is to be geographically representative and its membership should cover UN regions at least in the following way: five members from African and Asian States, one from Eastern European States, two from Latin American States, and two from Western European and Other States.

Once established, a WCI committee would draft its proposal and then formally register it with the WCI Administrative Board for collection of support. The report suggests that only such proposals should be eligible that are in line with the purposes of the UN Charter as stated in Article 1. Within this framework, proposals may have a broad scope. In particular, this includes being able to make reform proposals or propose changes to the UN Charter. Appeals against decisions of the WCI Administrative Board would be handled by an independent Ombudsperson.

The report recommends that a WCI would qualify for submission within 18 months after registration if it (1) collects the support of at least 0.5 percent of the population of each of ten UN member states following the same geographical criteria as above for the composition of WCI organising committees and (2) if an absolute threshold of five million signatures is reached. According to the report, anybody should be able to support a WCI and robust digital tools should be established to facilitate the collection of support. Verification would be undertaken based on random samples, residency information and date of birth.

The reports envisages that a successful WCI proposal will be placed automatically on the agenda of the General Assembly or the Security Council and that it obliges either of them to draft a resolution in response to the proposal and then to vote on this resolution. It is recommended that the WCI organising committee can make representations during the debate and that states are obliged to publish an 'explanation of the vote' whether they vote in favour of the resolution or not, in order to provide transparency to the WCI organisation committee.

Foreword

In 2020 the United Nations will commemorate its 75th anniversary under the theme "The future we want, the United Nations we need: reaffirming our collective commitment to multilateralism".[01] Many observers believe that the holistic and universal nature of the Agenda 2030 represents a global consensus on what the international community wishes to achieve within the next ten years. Thus, for the time being, full implementation of the Sustainable Development Goals could be the future we want.

The second part of the anniversary's theme is more tricky. With regards to the UN we need, a debate needs to be held. The world has changed significantly in the decades since the UN was established. It is necessary to take stock and examine what changes are required. From our point of view the UN is an indispensable centre for global deliberation, collaboration and action. The role of the UN as conscience keeper and upholder of universal norms and values remains steadfast. However, the notion of multilateralism needs to evolve beyond purely intergovernmental engagement.

A commitment to multilateralism at present should acknowledge more than ever that the UN's success depends on strong partnerships with major groups and stakeholders across the world. As the Earth Summit 2012 stated, sustainable development requires their meaningful involvement and active participation in processes that contribute to decision-making, planning and implementation of policies and programmes at all levels.[02] With the present report we wish to go a step further. Unfortunately, there is no formal UN instrument to enable individual citizens to influence its work. The UN we need and the UN we want welcomes and seeks the input of "We the Peoples" in whose name it was established 75 years ago. A global organization that wishes to leave no one behind – as member states pledged when they adopted the Agenda 2030[03] – needs to include everyone. In fact, the UN General Assembly has repeatedly stated the "right to equitable participation of all, without any discrimination, in domestic and global decision-making".[04]

This report recommends the creation of a World Citizens' Initiative to help make this happen. This instrument will enable global citizens to submit proposals to the UN General Assembly or the UN Security Council if they manage to collect sufficient support from fellow citizens across the world. Similar mechanisms exist in many countries at the national or sub-national levels. An important example this report draws upon is the European Citizens' Initiative, the first transnational instrument of this kind, to help explain in detail how a World Citizens' Initiative would function. Certainly, many technical details need to be discussed further and political will mobilized. Still, we emphasize the observation in this report that a World Citizens' Initiative is feasible and that all challenges can be overcome in the interests of the participation of "We the Peoples."

We are convinced that the UN, member states, civil society and global citizens alike will benefit from the direct connection a World Citizens' Initiative will establish, and that its creation will represent an important step forward for the UN. Clearly, a World Citizens' Initiative is a proposal that is complementary to other ongoing efforts such as the inclusion of major groups and civil society in the UN's work or the establishment of a United Nations Parliamentary Assembly.

The World Citizens' Initiative is a proposal that is in line with the concept of people-centered multilateral cooperation in a spirit of global citizenship.05 It may be a key element in the long-sought re-vitalization of the UN General Assembly. We urge representatives of UN member states to study this report and to launch an open and inclusive preparatory process for the establishment of a UN World Citizens' Initiative. We invite civil society groups and individuals to join the international Campaign for a UN World Citizens' Initiative and to provide their own comments and thoughts on the recommendations and reflections put forward in this report.

On behalf of the Campaign for a UN World Citizens' Initiative

Andreas Bummel, Executive Director,
Democracy Without Borders

Bruno Kaufmann, Board Member,
Democracy International

Lysa John, Secretary-General,
CIVICUS: World Alliance for Citizen Participation

Abbreviations

ECI	*European Citizens' Initiative*
ECOSOC	*Economic and Social Council of the UN*
EU	*European Union*
ICCPR	*International Covenant on Civil and Political Rights*
MEP	*Member of the European Parliament*
NGO	*Non-Governmental Organization*
TEU	*Treaty on European Union*
UN	*United Nations*
WCI	*World Citizens' Initiative*

Introduction

Traditionally, discussion of democratic legitimacy and proposals for new forms of democracy have focussed on state or sub-state level governance structures. However, in the context of globalisation and increased co-operation in issues that were formerly under the exclusive competence of the state, international institutions have in recent times significantly expanded the scope of their operations, taking action in response to an increasing range of global issues: from peace, economics and humanitarian affairs, to trade and environmental matters. As a result of this expansion, international institutions increasingly exercise power in a way that has a significant (often negative) impact upon individuals. Manifested in concerns about 'governance without government',[06] the increasing normative influence of autonomous international institutions – from the World Trade Organization, the International Monetary Fund, to the United Nations in particular – has triggered a marked change in attitudes among states, scholars and wider civil society. We thus note a shift in emphasis towards the consideration of the question of democratic legitimacy beyond the state, and particularly with reference to international institutions.[07] Indeed, the democratic deficit of international law and global governance has been called 'one of the central questions – perhaps the central question – in contemporary world politics'.[08] This move towards democratisation of international law and global governance regimes is part of a so-called third democratic transformation[09] and reflects the reduction in the autonomy of nation-states in an increasingly inter-connected world.

One of the organising assumptions in this report is that the UN should attempt to develop its democratic legitimacy and that this is possible, whilst recognising that there are inherent difficulties in implementing democracy in a new political environment such as the UN. De Burca has proposed a 'democratic striving approach', which supports the presumption that international organisations can and should be democratically legitimised:

Although the dominant model of democracy cannot simply be transposed from the national domain, we can and should try to translate the core values of democracy into a realizable institutional form when designing or reforming transnational governance practices. The democratic striving approach takes as its initial building block the principle of fullest possible participation by and representation of all those concerned with a commitment to ensuring the public-regarding nature of the process.[10]

The distinction between representation and participation highlighted by De Burca above is central to democratic debates at all levels of governance, including those relating to democratic reform of global governance.

From the representation perspective, a move towards democratisation may be premised on the idea of the 'sovereign equality of states' (UN Charter, Article 2(1)). Within the plenary organ of the UN General Assembly, for example, each UN member state is represented, and decision-making operates through a system of 'one state one vote'. This provides a degree of *representative* democracy at the international level.[11] However, with this understanding of representation beyond the nation-state being rooted in a traditional state-centric paradigm of international law, it can only take the debate so far. As Peters has articulated, 'global governance is transitively democratically legitimate only to the extent that international bodies are accountable through states to citizens'.[12] In this light, interest has turned more recently to the idea of a World Parliamentary Assembly, as a citizen-elected global representative institution,[13] and participation as a means of democratising global governance in, for example, a global citizens assembly.[14] This report contributes to this debate about how we might develop the participation of global citizens by examining the legal feasibility of establishing a World Citizens' Initiative (WCI). Democratic participatory instruments of this type are used at the member state level in several regions of the world. The proposal is that a citizens' initiative is adapted to the context of the UN to enable global citizens to launch and support policy proposals. Once organisers of a WCI have gathered sufficient support, the proposal would be put on the agenda of one of the principal political organs of the UN: the General Assembly or, if the initiative concerned the maintenance of international peace and security, the Security Council. The overall conclusion of the report is that the establishment of a WCI mechanism would be both legally feasible and politically beneficial for global democracy generally, and for the UN in particular.

The proposal to implement a WCI is split into the following five sections. First, several examples are given of existing mechanisms for individual participation in global governance structures. Second, some challenges to the formalisation of direct citizen participation in UN agenda-setting are acknowledged, and some comments are made about how these challenges might be qualified. Third, a general definition of citizens' initiatives is provided, and the basis for the democratic value of a citizens' initiative is explained. The fourth section comments on lessons to be learnt from the experience of the ECI. In the final section, the report offers a legal framework for the establishment of a WCI, which is split into three phases: the registration of a WCI, collecting support, and the submission of a successful initiative.

Citizen participation at the international level

The ongoing discussions pertaining to increased participation at the international level have focussed on the role of civil society. The importance of civil society in global governance was acknowledged at the 'We the Peoples Millennium Forum of 2000',[15] and at the 2002 Sustainable Development Summit, in particular.[16] In his 'Millennium Report', former UN Secretary-General Kofi Annan stated that the UN:

Must be opened up further to the participation of many actors whose contributions are essential to managing the path of globalization. Depending on the issues in hand, this may include civil society organizations, the private sector, parliamentarians, local authorities, scientific associations, educational institutions and many others.[17]

Furthermore, in resolutions on the '[p]romotion of a democratic and equitable international order', the General Assembly has repeatedly emphasised that achieving such an order would require the realisation of the 'right to equitable participation of all, without any discrimination, in domestic and global decision-making'.[18] The expert report on the UN's relations to civil society (Cardoso Report) outlined the 'deficits of democracy in global governance', and noted that '[o]ne of the key principles of representative democracy is connecting citizens to the decisions that affect them and ensuring public accountability for those decisions'.[19] Importantly, the Cardoso Report specifically emphasised the potential role of the UN in this regard, arguing that it should be at the centre of any efforts to 'reshape' democracy to make it more relevant to today's global realities and needs.[20]

In this light, in recent years, individuals have obtained some limited, formal participatory opportunities within global governance regimes. A good example is the compliance-control of the Aarhus Convention on environmental information. The compliance committee may receive communications brought forward by NGOs and individuals.[21] Another international complaint mechanism available to individuals is the World Bank Inspection Panel. Groups of two or more individuals who believe they have been negatively impacted by World Bank-financed projects can request an inspection. The Panel examines whether a failure of the World Bank to follow its own operational policies and procedures or contractual documents during the design, appraisal, or implementation of a project has adversely affected the material rights or interests of those persons.[22] In these procedures, the individual petitioners also have participatory rights.[23] Additionally, in international criminal proceedings before the International Criminal Court, victims have the right to participate in the proceedings and enjoy a limited right to be informed of the progress of the criminal trial.[24] Each of these examples envisages individuals participating retrospectively, as opposed to having the competence to proactively influence the UN's policy agenda.

Preliminary challenges

However, there are at least three principal challenges to implementing direct citizen participation in UN policymaking. The first challenge is practical in nature. With a constituency of 7.7 billion people, it is difficult for citizens to directly influence policy agendas or decision-making. Traditionally, democratic theory has been sceptical of the possibility of large-scale democracy.[25] However, developments in democratic theory, particularly in participatory and deliberative democratic literature, have recognised its feasibility in recent years. Dahl, for example, accepted the possibility of large-scale democracy beyond the state in his later writing.[26] At a practical level, the development of EU democracy has been an important demonstration of the possibility of reconceptualising democracy beyond the nation-state. Of most relevance to this report is the introduction of the ECI in 2012. This demonstrated the possibility of using participatory instruments at a supranational level and is an example, therefore, of how to enable citizens to influence global policy through the UN.

The second challenge relates to the general nature of the international legal system. States are the primary actors in international law.[27] Individuals are still considered as 'an object on which to bestow or recognize rights, not as agents from whom emanates the power to do such bestowing ... as an object or, at best, as a consumer of outcomes, but not as an agent of processes'.[28] Individuals cannot conclude treaties, and their behaviour does not constitute relevant practice which could lead to the formation of customary international law. Although individuals have rights and obligations, in a system based on the consent and mutual reciprocity of individual nation-states, there is no formal role for the individual in the law-making process. That said, there is some evidence to suggest that a broad interpretation of the right to political participation as guaranteed in Article 25 ICCPR might circumvent this doctrinal problem. The logical legal consequence of the citizens' right to political participation in global governance is that individuals are upgraded from mere passive international legal subjects (as holders of rights and bearers of obligations) to active international legal subjects. The legally relevant difference is that passive subjects are only capable of having rights, whereas active legal subjects are capable of creating law.[29] In this context, it has been argued that 'the international human right to political participation includes ... the right to contribute to the creation of international law'.[30]

The third challenge relates, more specifically, to the institutional architecture of the UN. The traditional anxiety regarding the distance between rulers and ruled is further exaggerated at the UN level. Notwithstanding the invocation of 'We the Peoples of the United Nations' in the preamble of the UN Charter, there remains no formal role for non-governmental actors of any kind in the work of the primary organs of the UN. The UN is exclusively composed of states and there are no bodies in which individual citizens are formally represented. A common point of departure when thinking through these questions is Article 71 of the UN Charter.[31] Article 71 is the only provision of the Charter which applies to NGOs. It grants the Economic and Social Council (ECOSOC) the competence to 'make suitable arrangements for consultation with non-governmental organizations'. As a result, many NGOs enjoy 'consultative status' on the ECOSOC. NGOs with general consultative status,[32] and NGOs with special consultative status,[33] may propose items for the Council's provisional agenda,[34] their representatives may attend public meetings of the ECOSOC Commission and its subsidiary organs as observers,[35] and they may submit written statements.[36] NGOs listed on the Roster, who make 'occasional ... contributions to the work of the Council or its subsidiary bodies or other UN bodies within their competence', may also fulfil these functions when matters being discussed fall within their field of competence, and upon the recommendation of the Secretary-General and at the request of the Commission may be heard by the Commission.[37] It is important to note, however, that even under this regime NGOs do not enjoy equal standing with states. The right of consultation does not amount to a right of participation. Instead, it is directed towards assisting ECOSOC to fulfil its mandate.[38] It is also confined, of course, to the areas of competence covered by ECOSOC's mandate. That said, the fact that the Charter itself acknowledges the possibility of entities other than states enjoying a formally recognised status in the UN provides a springboard to consider how this might apply in other contexts.

The democratic value of citizens' initiatives

Democracy at its core is based on popular sovereignty and political equality. This is the belief that all people affected by decisions should have an equal and effective opportunity to influence them. What this means in practice and how we recognise when these principles are sufficiently met is the subject of much debate. The democratic criteria of Robert Dahl underpin the analysis in this report.[39] He established five democratic criteria 'from within the enormous and often impenetrable thicket of ideas about democracy': effective participation, voting equality, gaining enlightened understanding, exercising final control over the agenda, and the inclusion of adults.[40] These characteristics are the democratic attributes that need to be in place for the members of a political system to be politically equal in determining the policies of the association. The introduction of the WCI aims to strengthen the extent to which the UN meets some of these criteria and enhance its democratic legitimacy.

Democratic instruments such as the WCI are the institutionalisation of participatory democracy and therefore, by definition, relate to increased and more effective participation. This, in turn, is expected to strengthen the democratic legitimacy of a polity or an international organisation such as the UN.[41] For this participation to be meaningful though, it also needs to tangibly influence policy decisions. This means that analysis of a citizens' initiative focuses on Dahls' criteria of inclusion, effective participation and exercising final control over the agenda. These fall into two categories in terms of their specific relevance to an evaluation of the implementation of a World Citizens' Initiative: inclusion and process, and impact.[42] *Inclusion* addresses the question of who participates; *process* the question of how citizens participate; and *impact* the question of what happens after citizens participate.[43]

Inclusion and process are linked because they both focus on the effectiveness of the participation opportunity that the WCI gives to citizens. Having an inclusive opportunity for all citizens to engage in institutional decision-making that affects them has long been an essential criterion for democracy, and this requirement of inclusion is important in all concepts of democracy, even elitist ones.[44] The WCI needs to increase the number and range of citizen voices directly heard in UN decision-making to increase UN democratic legitimacy. To maximise this, the design of the WCI should ensure that all citizens are able to use it to place issues on the UN political agenda in an equal and inclusive manner. In other words, no citizens should be excluded directly or indirectly from using the WCI, and all citizens should be treated equally when they try to organise or support a WCI. This is a significant challenge when trying to develop democracy on a global scale. Effective participation also means that the burden and barriers in terms of procedural complexity and resources that it imposes on citizens, as both organisers and supporters, such as funding, time, numerical thresholds etc., are kept to a minimum. The design of the WCI must minimise any restrictions it places on citizens' ability to take up this democratic opportunity.[45]

A citizens' initiative is a form of direct democracy that enables citizens to influence political decision-making, through placing an issue on the political agenda and triggering an institutional response, once a defined level of support has been reached.[46] Broadly speaking, there are two categories of citizens' initiatives.[47] Full-scale citizens' initiatives oblige a political institution to act,[48] often by holding a public vote, such as in Switzerland and California. The more common agenda-setting citizens' initiatives place an issue on the agenda of a sitting political body, usually the parliament of a state, but leave the final decision about how to respond to that institution.[49] The expectation is that the WCI will be an agenda-setting initiative because of the non-binding nature of the decisions of the UN General Assembly,[50] as is reflected in the repetition of the word recommendation in Articles 10, 11, 12, 13 and 14 of the UN Charter. The significance of an agenda-setting initiative is not therefore in the obligation to initiate a legal process, but in the political influence that citizens can exert through the citizen' initiative process.

The two elements of impact are: influencing the political agenda and influencing the subsequent decision-making. The first element relates to ensuring that citizens can use the WCI to place items on the UN agenda for discussion. Without this opportunity, the WCI would be a token gesture controlled by the institutions that control the agenda. In the case of the UN, the WCI would need to influence the agenda of the General Assembly or the Security Council. The second aspect, if an instrument such as the WCI is to strongly influence the UN's democratic legitimacy, is for participation through the WCI to have an influence over UN resolutions.

In the next section, the report focuses on the experience of the ECI. The report then concludes with an analysis of the three key stages of a citizens' initiative campaign, and the design features in them, such as the support threshold and the obligation that a WCI imposes. The analysis of citizens' initiatives that is presented and the proposals made for the implementation of a WCI are based on the principles outlined above; namely that citizen participation using the WCI should be inclusive, minimise barriers to participation, and should have an impact on the UN's political agenda and the decisions it makes.

The European Citizens' Initiative

Citizens' initiatives are well-established as state-level democratic instruments,[51] but the only transnational application is the ECI, which is a major democratic innovation introduced following the EU's Lisbon Treaty in 2008. It acts as an example for all transnational organisations struggling with criticisms of their democratic legitimacy. The ECI provides the closest applicable example for introducing a citizens' initiative into the UN governance structure and is evidence that a WCI reporting to the UN could succeed.

The potential significance of the ECI for EU democratic legitimacy is widely recognised,[52] and, upon its inception, the European Commission believed that it would be 'a significant step forward in the democratic life of the Union' and add a 'whole new dimension of participatory democracy'.[53] These high expectations have only been partly met, however, and there have been challenges to overcome. For example, the Commission initially took a cautious approach to ECI proposals that limited the numbers of ECIs,[54] there have been administrative and practical barriers to overcome,[55] and campaigners are concerned about the impact of successful ECIs.[56] Despite these challenges, the dozens of ECIs launched have mobilised millions of citizens and ECI proposals have influenced EU policy-making. The ECI, therefore, provides a positive basis on which to propose a World Citizens Initiative. In the same way that the idea of a World Parliamentary Assembly can draw some inspiration and best practice from regional parliamentary bodies,[57] the WCI can draw on the experience of the ECI.

The ECI is an example of an agenda-setting initiative that invites, rather than obliges, the European Commission to propose an EU legal act. The ECI has had an influence on political debate and the policy agenda, but it has had a limited concrete impact on EU law or policy. In other words, the ECI is closer to being an instrument of incumbent rather than critical democracy that can challenge policy to some degree, but its impact remains controlled by the existing institutions.[58] Expectations would have to also be carefully managed in relation to the WCI because the WCI legal framework, as is the case for the ECI, would oblige a formal response from the UN institutions, but would not oblige the UN to pass a resolution on the WCI proposal. Ultimately, the final decision as to what political impact a successful WCI could have rests with the UN members states. The impact of the WCI, therefore, would largely depend on the political influence that it could bring to bear rather than its legal strength.

The ECI regulations and process set the context for discussion of a WCI. Art 11(4) Treaty of European Union establishes the European Citizens Initiative as an opportunity for citizens to invite the Commission to make a proposal for a legal act:

Not less than one million citizens who are nationals of a significant number of member states may take the initiative of inviting the European Commission, within the framework of its powers, to submit any appropriate proposal on matters where citizens consider that a legal act of the Union is required for the purpose of implementing the Treaties.[59]

The phrases highlighted above in Art 11(4) establish the treaty basis for the support thresholds, the ECI's strength of legal obligation, and the limits on the subject matter of the ECI.[60] These are the key characteristics that define the scope and type of citizens' initiative for the ECI.[61] A successful ECI needs support from 1 million citizens from across the EU, it can invite but not oblige the Commission to start the legislative process, and an ECI proposal can relate to any EU competence where citizens think reform is needed.[62] The WCI design also needs to consider these issues raised by the text highlighted in Art 11(4) TEU. A decision needs to be taken about the number of citizens and states that represent a level of legitimacy that can trigger a response from the UN General Assembly or Security Council; what response is obliged from these bodies; and what proposals are appropriate for a WCI. Art 11(4) was implemented by Regulation 211/2011, which defined these characteristics in more detail,[63] and established the ECI process.[64] The report discusses below how this translates to a WCI process whose proposals would be presented to the UN, and in light of the criteria described above relating to Inclusion and Process, and Impact.

Implementing the World Citizens' Initiative

Step 1: Establishing a citizens' initiative

The Committee

The first formal step for a citizens' initiative is to establish an organising committee that will take responsibility for the citizens' initiative process. This committee is formed for two broad purposes: planning and leading the campaign for the collection of support for the citizens' initiative proposal, and the dissemination of the ideas within the proposal. As the European Parliament stated in relation to requiring the establishment of a committee for each ECI: the committee is 'to encourage the emergence of European-wide issues and to foster reflection on those issues'.[65] The WCI committee would, similarly, be tasked with ensuring that the proposal reaches a global audience.

Secondly, the committee is responsible for ensuring the initiative follows procedures appropriately. An understanding and implementation of the relevant legal framework and funding transparency are needed during the life of a citizens' initiative campaign. As the European Parliament stated: the nomination of a lead person from the committee is "for the sake of transparency and smooth and efficient communication".[66] Similarly, a WCI would need a lead contact for liaison with the UN.

The WCI committee members would serve as the data controllers of the information collected within the statements of support given by citizens, and therefore they are legally responsible for the security of the data. Committee members are also responsible for the publication of information about any funding received to ensure transparency of the supporters of an initiative. These legal requirements could be problematic for a WCI that has a global reach and operates within many different legal jurisdictions. One possibility is that the UN itself takes on responsibility for these issues as far possible – for example by providing the IT infrastructure for storing information and agreeing on a legal jurisdiction under which this is held. The WCI could also allow organising committees to have a legal personality to reduce liability issues.

An ancillary purpose of the WCI committee is to increase the extent to which a proposal starts with wide geographical support. The ECI requires the formation of an organising committee of at least 7 EU citizens, resident in 7 different member states, prior to the application to register an ECI. To increase the extent to which the WCI reflects the interests of a global audience, it is recommended that the composition of the organising committees for WCIs contain at least 10 people. The composition of the committee should comply with the principle of 'equitable geographical distribution' set out in Article 23(1) of the Charter. General Assembly Resolution 1991 (XVIII), adopted in 1963, formally apportions non-permanent seats on the Security Council, for example, according to a specific geographical 'pattern'. The geographical pattern set out in the resolution, and which WCI organising committees should reflect, is as follows:

(a) five African and Asian States;
(b) one Eastern European States;
(c) two Latin American States;
(d) two Western European and Other States.[67]

In order to ensure genuine geographical representation, the scenario whereby the committee is made up of representatives of five Asian states, or five African states, with no representation from the other region, should be avoided. The only minor change to the pattern that is recommended, therefore, is that there should be an explicit requirement that three Asian states are represented, and two African states. Considering the rationale underpinning the establishment of a WCI, that is, enhanced citizen participation, the considerably larger population of Asian states compared to African states should be acknowledged.

It is also recommended that the organising committee is made up of 'natural persons'. In other words, the members of the committee cannot be politicians or formal representatives of civil society organisations. This would serve to increase the WCI's status as an initiative for citizens and not corporate or political interests and reduce the chance of lobby capture. However, in practice, given the global reach of a WCI and the resource requirements this implies, it is likely that civil society organisations will play a central role in the WCI campaigns, as they do for the ECI.

Initiative Registration

Having established a committee, the WCI organisers need to draft their proposal and then register it for collection of support. The amount and type of information that organisers need to submit at registration vary greatly between citizens' initiatives. Clarity is important so that citizens and the UN institutions understand the proposal, but excessive requirements will act as a barrier to participation. The ECI takes a relatively light-touch approach, only requiring the title of the ECI and a brief explanation of its subject matter and aims. The authors recommend that WCI proposals should be more detailed and presented as a draft General Assembly or Security Council resolution, depending on which body's competence the proposal falls under. This will provide clarity in terms of the proposal and increase the certainty in terms of the expected outcome of a WCI process that has to reach a global audience, but it is worth noting that this could mean that WCI organisers need to seek legal advice to help write the draft resolution.

The next step in a citizens' initiative process is the formal registration of the initiative. At this point, there will typically be an eligibility check to make sure the citizens' initiative proposal meets certain criteria. Usually, these will require that the proposal is appropriate and within the powers of the institution that will receive a successful citizens' initiative proposal. The review of citizens' initiative proposals at registration though should not excessively limit the public discourse a citizens' initiative proposal can develop. On the other hand, it is important that organisers of a citizens' initiative are clear from the outset whether their proposal could have the desired impact, and whether legally the institution receiving the citizens' initiative proposal can make the policy change requested.

The eligibility check for the ECI has four criteria: 1 – forming the committee, 2 – the proposal in the ECI must not be 'manifestly outside the framework of the Commission's powers to propose a legal act', 3 – the ECI is not manifestly abusive, frivolous or vexatious, and 4 – is not manifestly contrary to the values of the Union. This report recommends that the UN establish a similar registration process that ensures a WCI proposal meets the procedural requirements, is within the competence of the UN, and fits within the principles of the UN.

The most controversial registration criteria for the ECI is point 2. The hybrid supranational/intergovernmental nature of the EU and the fact that EU laws are directly applicable in its member states means this question of competence creep is a particular concern for the EU's member states. The Commission was over-zealous in guarding against this problem in the early years of the ECI.[68] They refused to register a high percentage of ECIs through an overly strict registration review of proposals that decided they were outside the powers of the Commission. The competences of the UN General Assembly, however, are not legally binding on the member state so this question of citizen participation increasing the control of the supranational organisation over the member states should be less of an issue for a citizens' initiative presented to the UN. The competences of the UN General Assembly are also very wide-reaching, and so the competence check at registration should be straightforward assuming that WCI proposals are welcome on all issues that are within the competence of the UN General Assembly.

One important decision taken by the UN committee at registration is whether the WCI falls within the competence of the UN General Assembly or the UN Security Council. The process for proposals that are within the competence of either body is the same up to the point of presentation of a successful WCI. The obligation imposed on the Security Council and the General Assembly after that differ and are discussed in section 4 below.

The other criteria for ECI registration have not led to any ECIs being refused registration and should not raise any issues for a WCI. The forming of the committee is a simple procedural check. The experience of the ECI indicates that the question of whether a WCI proposal is malicious, frivolous or vexatious is likely to only arise on very rare occasions. The administrative organ of the UN would need to make a judgment on those occasions. In order to make this judgment, the organ should be driven, first and foremost, by the purposes of the UN Charter as stated in Article 1. It is logical that the registration criteria should mirror the founding purposes of the organisation that will receive the proposal. Article 1(3) which emphasises the importance of 'promoting and encouraging respect for human rights and for fundamental freedoms for all without distinction as to race, sex, language, or religion', will be particularly relevant. The fundamental principles of the Universal Declaration of Human Rights may also be taken into consideration at this point. Only those proposed initiatives that would manifestly run contrary to the purposes of the UN would not meet this criterion. For these reasons, the registration of a WCI is unlikely to be a burdensome process for the UN administration or for organisers. This is beneficial in democratic terms because it allows a wider range of issues to be debated publicly and placed on the political agenda, and means there is a low barrier to entry for starting the democratic process. This sort of 'light-touch' registration approach is also easier to justify for an agenda-setting initiative such as the WCI that has little legal obligation built-in because there is little risk to the overall political environment or to fundamental rights.

In short, the lower the barriers at registration, the more citizens will use the WCI and the more impact it is likely to have on the democratic legitimacy of the UN through increasing inclusivity and citizen influence over and decision-making

One final substantive question is whether a WCI should be able to advance reform proposals or charter changes. Using the ECI to propose a fundamental change to the EU treaties is a controversial question and one that is not clearly resolved by the law establishing the ECI in Art 11(4). On the one hand, it is argued that an ECI is unlikely to ever have the level of support that would legitimise a request to change fundamental law and that it is the states that are members of the EU and responsible for initiating change to the EU treaties. On the other hand, it is argued that the ECI process endows a right on citizens through their EU citizenship, rather than their member state citizenship, and so citizens should be entitled to use the ECI to propose a change to all EU laws, including the treaties themselves. Also, to exclude proposals that require treaty change is to exclude some of the most important EU political issues from the scope of the ECI, which substantially limits the democratic value of this instrument. Moreover, the fact that the

ECI obliges just a political response to a proposal and is only an agenda-setting instrument means that it would only have an impact on the treaties where the other EU institutions agreed with the proposal. The recommendation is therefore that the WCI has a broad scope that includes being able to make reform proposals or propose changes to the UN charter. Given the controversy this issue is likely to raise, the WCI framework should make it clear that this is possible.

Registration Administration

The WCI implies administrative discretion, requires policy oversight of the WCI implementation, and the process itself requires administrative oversight. For example, an entity would be required to ensure that WCI registration decisions meet the required criteria (see discussion above), and later in the process, verification of signatures. The WCI will, therefore, necessitate the establishment of a new organ of the UN. For ease, the new organ will be referred to as the 'WCI Administrative Board'.

Of course, the Board could be established through a treaty between member states of the UN. The treaty would set out an explicit institutional relationship with the General Assembly, but the organ would not be categorised as a subsidiary organ. Another option is that the General Committee administers the process. The General Committee is a microcosm of the General Assembly, to which the President of the General Assembly, the twenty-one Vice-Presidents of the General Assembly, as well as the chairpersons of each of the six main committees, belong.[69] The General Committee is responsible for organising the work of the session and for recommending to the General Assembly the scheduling and handling of each item on the agenda. For this option, the General Assembly would have to amend its Rules of Procedure to establish a WCI instrument and provisions for its management.

A third option, which the authors recommend, is the establishment of the WCI Administrative Board as a new organ with sole competency in this area. Article 7(2) of the Charter generally provides for the establishment of subsidiary organs by the principal organs of the United Nations. Under Article 22 of the UN Charter, 'the General Assembly may establish such subsidiary organs as it deems necessary for the performance of its functions'. The decision to establish a subsidiary organ may be viewed as an 'important decision', per Article 18(2). If this was the case, it would require a two-thirds majority rather than a simple majority. However, it is debatable whether this would be required. In most cases, the General Assembly requires consensus and a roll-call vote does not tend to be taken. However, considering the democratic role of the WCI, our recommendation would be that the original founding act of establishing the WCI Administrative Board have this minimalist requirement of democratic legitimacy.

Subsidiary organs are essentially characterised by three features, which speak to only a limited autonomy:

1. *Subsidiary organs are created by a principal organ of the UN;*
2. *the membership, structure and terms of the subsidiary organ are determined and modified by the principal organ;*
3. *subsidiary organs may be terminated or suspended by a principal organ.*[70]

However, the subsidiary organ would necessarily possess a certain degree of independence, since otherwise, the entity would simply be a part of the principal organ.[71] In this light, Szasz identifies a category of 'quasi-autonomous bodies'.[72] The WCI Administrative Board might potentially be best viewed in this light. It is important that the Board maintains a degree of independence from the very institution that WCI's will be established to influence.

In general, the initiative for establishing subsidiary organs comes from the General Assembly itself. Interestingly though, the General Assembly has also founded subsidiary organs on the recommendation of international conferences. For example, the United Nations Environment Programme was initiated by a recommendation of the Conference on the Human Environment in Stockholm in 1972. NGOs played a pivotal role in the drafting of the Stockholm Declaration and the Action Plan for Human Environment which were instrumental in lobbying the General Assembly to act. The World Food Council was also established in 1974 by the General Assembly on the recommendation of the World Food Conference.[73]

Although negative registration decisions are likely to be rare, there may still be times when WCI organisers may want to appeal against registration decisions. The ECI registration appeals go to the Court of Justice of the EU.[74] There is no comparable primary organ in the UN, so an independent adjudicatory process would need to be set up. Our recommendation is to establish an independent Ombudsperson office, similar to the UN Office of the Ombudsperson, which was established in 2009 to mitigate unfairness to individuals in UN Security Council sanctions decision-making.[75] The

Ombudsperson is not an adjudicatory process but instead fulfils a fact-finding inquisitorial role that examines maladministration. Upon receipt of a request of delisting, the Ombudsperson engages in a four-month period of information gathering. At the end of this process, the Ombudsperson prepares a report outlining the information she has received and lays out the main arguments relating to the request. If the Ombudsperson recommends delisting, the individual will be removed from the list unless, within sixty days, the Sanctions Committee decides to maintain the listing. The Committee is obliged to give reasons for rejecting the request.[76] A similar process that focuses on administrative issues, such as the duty to give reasons, could be followed in relation to appeals against WCI registration decisions.

Step 2: Collecting support

Once registered, a citizens' initiative can start the process of collecting support for its proposal. ECI organisers have 18 months to collect the requisite level of support. The organisers inform the Commission of the start date, which must be within 3 months of the ECI registration decision.[77]

Support threshold

The support threshold is the most complicated aspect of this phase of a citizens' initiative. The success threshold for a citizens' initiative is the point at which the political body has decided that the proposal has the legitimacy to influence their decision-making. The higher the level of support required, the more legitimate it is for a citizens' initiative to have an impact on decision-making.

If set too low, the legitimacy of a citizens' initiative proposal will be limited and reduce the chance that unwilling political actors will respond to a proposal that is put to them, even if it meets the threshold. However, the higher the threshold is set and the more complicating factors that are included, the more it will act as a barrier and reduce the likelihood of the WCI being used.

The degree of obligation that a citizens' initiative can impose influences the threshold decisions. In general, the stronger the obligation that a citizens' initiative imposes, the higher the threshold for support. Higher support and greater legitimacy are needed to oblige a political institution to act. For example, in Hungary, there are three levels at which an initiative obliges action: an agenda initiative needs 50,000 signatures; at 100,000 signatures Parliament has to decide whether a binding or an advisory referendum is held; 200,000 signatures are required to initiate an obligatory and binding referendum.[78] As the WCI is a form of agenda-setting initiative, the threshold requirements at which a WCI would be submitted to the UN General Assembly or Security Council can be set relatively low.

The threshold also reflects the level of difficulty for organisers to collect the support needed. The ECI has to collect support from a relatively low percentage of the population when compared to national citizens' initiatives. This reflects, in part, the large geographical area that organisers need to reach. This issue would also arise for the WCI, and so setting a relatively low support threshold will be needed to avoid a prohibitively high level of difficulty for WCI organisers.

The threshold requirements must also reflect the sources of legitimacy for the political institution that a proposal is seeking to influence. The ECI threshold, for example, balances member state legitimacy with the supranational legitimacy of the number of citizens and reflects the fact that the EU is a hybrid intergovernmental/supranational polity. For national citizens' initiatives, the threshold is usually just an absolute number of national citizens, which reflects the nation-state as a single sovereign entity. This is not the case for the UN. As the UN is an intergovernmental organisation, the WCI would need to reflect support from a certain number of member states, perhaps also regions, to be legitimate. Setting a level of member state and regional support will also avoid WCI proposals coming from a relatively small geographical area. Again, though, if this number is too high, then it will become too difficult to collect support and the WCI will not be used. In part, this could be mitigated by setting a longer time period for collecting support. This report recommends that a WCI be given 18 months to try to collect the necessary level of support. Although this is still a challenging timeframe, any longer and the topicality and legitimacy of a proposal is reduced.

This report recommends that we use the same criteria as for the composition of the WCI organising committee to ensure geographical representativeness. We recommend that a WCI be presented to the UN when it has sufficient support from citizens from at least the following:

(a) five African and Asian States;
(b) one Eastern European State;
(c) two Latin American States;
(d) two Western European and Other States.[79]

This is the same as the pattern used for forming the organising committee. For a state to be quorate and count towards the WCI threshold, this report recommends that the WCI needs support from 0.5% of the population of that state. This places a WCI towards the lower end of national initiatives in terms of the percentage of support needed for a national citizens' initiative. The overall percentage of the world population supporting a WCI will be much lower than this, and lower than the 0.2% of the total EU population that the ECI needs. This approach treats all states equally. The ECI takes a different approach. It uses a sliding scale that means smaller states need a higher percentage of the population to be quorate in support of an ECI proposal than larger member states. This scale is based on the allocation of MEPs. The aim is to balance the influence of population size against influence as a member state through smaller states getting proportionately more MEPs than larger states. The ECI sliding scale reduces the temptation to seek support just from smaller member states. However, we do not recommend a sliding scale for the WCI because there is no pre-existing agreement to base the scale on, and more importantly, the UN works on a 'one state - one vote' principle in the General Assembly. A sliding scale of population support for states to be quorate for a WCI would run counter to this.

This report also recommends that an absolute level of support is required before a WCI proposal is presented to the UN. The UN does not need the transnational legitimacy that an absolute figure bestows for it to act, and there is no UN citizenship. However, the need for an absolute figure takes the WCI beyond the confines of the intergovernmental framing of the UN and its member state focus, and still confers extra legitimacy. It also helps maintain a balance between the value of larger and smaller states to the collection process... This report, therefore, recommends that a WCI get support from 5 million people before it can be presented to the UN institutions.

The European Parliament recognised the practical difficulties and potential costs of reaching the support thresholds for an ECI in a polity such as the EU and proposed a number of mitigating measures.[80] To this end, they requested the provision by the Commission of an online system for the collection of signatures,[81] a comprehensive user guide and a help desk for providing advice.[82] An EU data server and translation services have also been made available to organisers. It is suggested that the UN should establish a body to support citizens wishing to use the WCI process and help mitigate what can be a costly process with these types of services and initiatives. This body will need to offer the same level of support that ECI organisers are offered, and make sure that there is the highest level of data security for information collected from supporters of a WCI. Although a paper collection process should still be available, the online collection system is even more important for a global campaign to collect support for a WCI proposal and therefore warrants a high level of support.

Support Eligibility

Anybody should be able to support a WCI. For other citizens' initiatives, there is a political boundary that usually limits those who can support a proposal either based on residency or on citizenship. The UN has no such political boundary. The question is then how to identify the person supporting a WCI proposal. The ECI experience has highlighted the impact that excessive identity requirements can have on reducing the likelihood that someone will support a proposal.[83] This has led to a simplification of the identification requirements in the new ECI regulation that encourages residency as the basis for identification rather than identity documents that vary from state to state. The recommendation, therefore, would be that someone wishing to support a WCI should only be required to provide residency information and date of birth. This also simplifies the process to verify the support for WCI proposals, which the UN would need to establish. The most straightforward and proportionate process would be to verify a random sample of statements of support for a WCI proposal to make sure that they are real people and genuine supporters of the WCI proposal. The WCI process will also need digital tools to ensure that robots and multiple registrations cannot corrupt the collection of support. The UN will also need to decide whether verification is carried out by each state where citizens that support a proposal are resident, or whether they centralise the verification of support into a UN body.

Step 3: Submission and response

The final phase for a successful citizens' initiative is the submission of the proposal to a decision-making body. When designing a citizens' initiative this decision about the obligation that it imposes is key. One of the defining features of a citizens' initiative is that it imposes an obligation on a political body – otherwise it is merely a petition. The degree and type of obligation though vary significantly. In Finland, it obliges the Parliament to debate a proposal and make a legislative recommendation. In Switzerland, a citizens' initiative can oblige holding a referendum.

The ECI just obliges the Commission to explain its decision to act or not. This has led to something of an expectation gap between ECI campaigners and the Commission, with campaigners wanting full implementation of their proposals, and the Commission expecting a compromise with existing policy positions. The Water Directive was the first piece of EU legislation influenced by a successful ECI; the Right to Water ECI.[84] The Right to Water Campaigners though were hoping for further impact from their campaign. The 'One of Us' ECI campaign has gone as far as to ask for judicial review of the Commission's response to their ECI, which collected over two million signatures.[85] Without policy impact, there will be little incentive to use the WCI, but the expectations of campaigners also need to be managed to avoid disappointment with policy outcomes at the end of the political process and to avoid challenges to follow-up decisions. The proposals below try to strike this balance between political discretion and campaigner expectations.

WCI proposal within the competenceof General Assembly

For all matters other than international peace and security, the General Assembly is the most appropriate forum to discuss a WCI proposal. If the underlying rationale is to influence the political agenda and to encourage states to support a proposal, the General Assembly would be an ideal forum. The Assembly is 'essentially a debating chamber, a forum for the exchange of ideas and the discussion of a wide-ranging category of problems'.[86]

There are three options for placing a WCI proposal on the General Assembly agenda:

First, the WCI may be added to the agenda to be discussed at the initial general debate of each annual session while heads of state and government are present. This would require the organising committee to meet the required timescales and to comply with the procedures of the General Committee, the body responsible for setting the agenda.

Second, a WCI initiative might trigger a 'special session' of the General Assembly which can be called by the Secretary-General at the request of the Security Council or a majority of member states.[87]

Third, it may be that instead of a plenary debate, it would be preferable for the WCI proposal to be discussed in one of the six main committees that cover: disarmament and international security, economic and financial, social, humanitarian and cultural, special political and decolonisation; administrative and budgetary; and legal matters.

Further to this, this report recommends that a WCI obliges the UN, either the General Assembly or the Security Council, to draft a resolution in response to the proposal and then to vote on the resolution.

The action that a citizens' initiative can force also depends, of course, on the powers of the political body that it addresses. The UN General Assembly has the power to pass resolutions that member states are expected to respond to, but are not legally binding. It is itself a form of agenda-setting body. It is not a legislative or the executive body in the mould of a state. However, the General Assembly is in a position to launch intergovernmental negotiations under the auspices of the UN on new treaties or to put questions in front of the International Law Commission for further consideration, to name two relevant ways of taking action.

Furthermore, to organise a World citizens' initiative is a major undertaking. The effort that a successful citizens' initiative requires from citizens is an important consideration when deciding what obligation a citizens' initiative should impose on a political body. If there is a very little meaningful impact from a citizens' initiative then citizens are unlikely to use the instrument. This is particularly true for a global citizens' initiative that requires organisation across the world.

Excessive obligation from a citizens' initiative runs the risk of legitimacy issues. This is because a successful WCI will still only have a relatively small percentage of citizens that support a proposal. This is one of the reasons that states, such as Switzerland, hold a referendum after a citizens' initiative. A referendum provides a mandate from the whole population. The UN could take another approach to try to address this issue of legitimacy and complement the intergovernmental legitimacy for a WCI proposal from the UN process. The aim would be to gain further transnational legitimacy. Two possibilities are to establish a World Parliamentary Assembly that would debate WCI proposals or to form a global citizens' assembly.

The authors envisage that a WCI proposal will be placed automatically on the agenda of the General Assembly. It should be noted that this bypasses the traditional route through the General Committee, which decides upon the agenda for each upcoming session on an annual basis. A WCI proposal that is successful would be presented to fall in line with this annual agenda-setting process. This would require the organising committee to meet the required timescales and to comply with the procedures of the General Committee, the body responsible for setting the agenda.

It is recommended that the WCI organising committee can be represented, and make representations during the debate. Of course, the ultimate vote on whether the resolution should be adopted will be made by states. It would not be prudent to suggest a fundamental restructuring of the voting system of the General Assembly. The authors would recommend, however, that states are obliged to publish an 'explanation of the vote' in order to provide transparency to the WCI organisation committee.

WCI proposal within the competence of the Security Council

If the subject matter of the initiative related to the maintenance of international peace and security, the proposal would be submitted to the UN Security Council. The Security Council has 'primary responsibility for the maintenance of international peace and security'.[88] In carrying out this responsibility, member states agree that the Council is acting on their behalf. The potential value in submitting the proposal to the Security Council would be that decisions of the Council are, contrary to recommendations of the General Assembly, binding on all states in the international community.[89] The potential challenge, however, is that the capacity to impose binding enforcement measures is predicated on a determination by the Council that the situation in question constitutes either a 'threat to the peace, breach of the peace or an act of aggression'.[90] It is commonly accepted that this determination is a political question, and not easily subjected to objective legal criteria. It is also accepted that it is the Security Council, and the Council only, that is competent to make this decision. Representatives of the WCI organising committee may participate in the Security Council debates preceding this decision, however, they would not be permitted voting rights. The rules of procedure currently already allow for the participation of "specially affected" non-Council member states.[91] The WCI organising committee might, in this light, be seen as a 'specialised agency' along the lines of the relationship between non-governmental organisations and the Economic and Social Council. Support for this suggestion can be found in Article 70, which provides the 'arrangements for representatives of the specialized agencies to participate, without vote, in its deliberations'. In short, a successful WCI would oblige the Council to discuss its proposal, but it would not translate into an obligation to take definitive action. If the Council determines that a WCI does not fall into its purview, it may automatically be submitted to the General Assembly instead.

Conclusion: World Citizens' Initiative: Time to act

This report proposes a major evolution for transnational democracy: the introduction of a World Citizens' Initiative that will give global citizens the opportunity to directly influence UN policymaking. This report discusses some of the key considerations for those tasked with framing a World Citizen's Initiative. These are the registration criteria and scope of a WCI, the thresholds that need to be reached for a WCI to oblige a response from the UN, the principal technical requirements relating to the collection and verification of support, and the impact that a successful WCI should have. Also included are recommendations for some of the most important design decisions, and indicates some of the further tasks for the UN to establish a WCI. Although this report has focussed on the most important aspects of WCI, a number of other questions will, of course, arise when the details of WCI design are tackled, not least because of political considerations that are outside the scope of a legalistic report such as this one. Nevertheless, this report has shown that a WCI is feasible and will hopefully provide the impetus for the discussions that might lead to its establishment. Such a move would complement other existing mechanisms to enhance democratisation of global governance regimes generally, and citizens' participation in particular.

Annex

Campaign statement

At the launch of the Campaign for a UN World Citizens' Initiative on 14 November 2019 civil society organizations and individual citizens were invited to sign the following statement. To support the statement and to see a current list of endorsements visit the campaign's website at www.worldcitizensinitiative.org.

We the Peoples
It's time to give citizens a voice at the UN

The biggest challenges facing us such as climate change, violent conflict and inequality are global and cross cutting in nature. They need collective responses from the international community. The UN is the key arena to make this happen.

As the UN celebrates its 75th anniversary, it's time to give people a direct voice in its affairs. The UN's legitimacy, relevance and ability to tackle contemporary challenges can be enhanced by making it more open and accessible to ordinary citizens.

As global citizens and as representatives of civil society from around the world, we urge the UN to establish the instrument of a World Citizens' Initiative which will enable citizens to put forward proposals on key issues of global concern for discussion and further action at the highest political level. The UN should put any matter that reaches a certain threshold of support from people onto the agenda of the opening debate of each annual session of the General Assembly.

We firmly believe that the addition of the new instrument of a World Citizens' Initiative will enhance the agency of citizens all over the globe, empowering them, the UN and its member states alike to tackle global challenges in our increasingly complex and interconnected world more effectively.

The time has come to give a voice to citizens of the world and realize the promise of the Preamble of the UN Charter which begins with the words, "We the Peoples of the United Nations".

Add your support to our call and join our campaign! We are stronger together.

Endnotes

01 United Nations. Commemoration of the Seventy-Fifth Anniversary of the United Nations. UN Doc. A/RES/73/299, 14 June 2019.

02 United Nations. The Future We Want: Outcome Document of the United Nations Conference on Sustainable Development. UN Doc. A/RES/66/288, 27 July 2012. Para. 42ff.

03 United Nations. Transforming Our World: The 2030 Agenda for Sustainable Development. UN Doc. A/RES/70/1, 25 Sept. 2015. Preamble.

04 United Nations. Promotion of a Democratic and Equitable International Order. UN Doc. A/RES/59/193, 20 Dec. 2004. Para. 4 (h); see also latest resolution A/RES/73/169, para. 6 (h).

05 People-Centered Multilateralism: A Call to Action. 67th United Nations DPI NGO Conference, Aug. 2018.

06 JN Rosenau & E-O Czempiel (eds), Governance without Government: Order and Change in World Politics (Cambridge University Press 1992).

07 JS Nye, 'Globalization's Democratic Deficit: How to Make International Institutions More Accountable' (2001) 80(4) Foreign Affairs https://www.foreignaffairs.com/articles/2001-07-01/globalizations-democratic-deficit-how-make-international-institutions-more.

08 A Moravcsik, 'Is There a "Democratic Deficit" in World Politics? A Framework for Analysis' (2004) 39 Government and Opposition 336, 336.

09 R Dahl, Democracy and its Critics (Yale University Press 1989)

10 G De Burca, 'Developing Democracy Beyond the State' (2008) Columbia Journal of Transnational Law 221, 276-277.

11 See, generally, TD Zweifel, International Organizations and Democracy: Accountability, Politics, and Power (Lynne Rienner 2006).

12 A Peters, 'Dual Democracy' in J Klabbers, A Peters and G Ulfstein (eds), The Constitutionalization of International Law (Oxford University Press 2009) 263, 264.

13 Jo Leinen and Andreas Bummel, A World Parliament: Governance and Democracy in the 21st Century (Democracy Without Borders 2018); see also the Campaign for a UN Parliamentary Assembly <www.unpacampaign.org>

14 J Dryzek, A Bachtiger & A MIlewicz, 'Toward a Deliberative Global Citizens' Assembly' (2001) 2(1) Global Policy 33.

15 We the Peoples Millennium Forum Declaration and Agenda for Action, 'Strengthening the UN for the 21st Century' (26 May 2000) (UN Doc A/54/959). See in this document notably Part F: 'Strengthening and democratizing the United Nations and international organizations' which suggested that the UN should 'support the creation and funding of a Global Civil Society Forum to meet at least every two to three years in the period leading up to the annual session of the General Assembly, provided that such a forum is conducted democratically and transparently and is truly representative of all sectors of civil society and all parts of the world'.

16 Report of the World Summit on Sustainable Development (26 August--4 September 2002) UN Doc A/CONF.1999/20, at 64, section A(g), which listed as a key objective: 'Enhancing participation and effective involvement of civil society and other relevant stakeholders ... as well as promoting transparency and broad public participation'.

17 UN Secretary-General Kofi Annan, "We the Peoples': The Role of the United Nations in the 21st Century' (Millennium Report) (2000) at 13.

18 UN Human Rights Council Resolution 18/6, 'Promotion of a Democratic and Equitable International Order' (13 October 2011) UN Doc A/RES/72/172, para 6(h).

19 Report of the Panel of Eminent Persons on United Nations-Civil Society Relations, 'We the Peoples: Civil Society, the United Nations and Global Governance' ('Cardoso Report') UN Doc A/58/817 (11 June 2004), para 7.

20 Ibid, para 28.

21 UN Economic Commission for Europe, Decision I/7 Review of Compliance, Annex 'Structure and Functions of the Compliance Committee and Procedures for the Review of Compliance' (2002) Doc ECE/MP.PP/2/Add.8, at para 18.

22 Resolution Establishing the World Bank Inspection Panel (22nd September 1993) (IBRD Resolution No 93-10, IDA Resolution No 93-6).

23 World Bank Inspection Panel Operating Procedures, art 47.

24 See Art 68(3) ICC-Statute.

25 RA Dahl, 'Can International Organizations be Democratic? A Skeptic's View' in I Shapiro and C Hacker-Cordon (eds), Democracy's Edges (Cambridge University Press 1999) 19, 22: 'the opportunities available to the ordinary citizen to participate effectively in the decisions of a world government would diminish to the vanishing point'.

26 Dahl, Democracy and its Critics (n 4).

27 The most famous exposition of this approach remains that of Oppenheim: 'Since the law of nations is based on the common consent of individual States, States solely and exclusively are subjects of international law'. See LFL Oppenheim, International Law: A Treatise (2nd edn, Longmans, Green and Company 1912) 19. See also SS Lotus [1927] PICJ Rep Ser A 10, at 18: 'International law governs relations between independent States'.

28 JHH Weiler 'The Geology of International Law -- Governance, Democracy and Legitimacy' (2004) 64 Zeitschrift für ausländisches öffentliches Recht und Völkerrecht 547, 558.

29 Peters (n 7) 300.

30 A Peters, 'Membership in the Global Constitutional Community' in J Klabbers, A Peters and G Ulfstein (eds), The Constitutionalization of International Law (Oxford University Press 2009) 153, 161.

31 See, generally, S Hobe, 'Article 71' in B Simma, The Charter of the United Nations: A Commentary (3rdedn, vol 2, Oxford University Press, 2012) 1788; C Algar, 'The Emerging Roles of NGOs in the UN System: From Article 71 to a People's Millennium Assembly' (2002) 8 Global Governance 93.

32 'organizations that are concerned with most of the activities of the Council', ECOSOC Res 1993/31 (1993).

33 'organizations that have a special competence in ... only a few fields of activity covered by the Council', ECOSOC Res 1996/31 (1996), at para 23.

34 Ibid, at para 34.

35 Ibid, at para 35.

36 Ibid, at para 36.

37 Ibid, at para 38.

38 Ibid, at para 18.

39 Robert Dahl, the preeminent democratic theorist of the 20th century, set out five criteria in Dahl, Democracy and its Critics (n 4).

40 First set out in his book Dahl, Democracy and its Critics (n 4). Quoted here from R Dahl, On Democracy, YUP (2000) 38-39.

41 Dahl defines effective participation in the following way: "Before a policy is adopted by the association, all the members must have equal and effective opportunities for making their view known to the other members as to what the policy should be" in R Dahl, On Democracy (Yale University Press 2000) 37.

42 This reflects the input, throughput and output approach to democracy but is not directly derived from that strand of literature, e.g. V Schmidt, 'Democracy and Legitimacy in the European Union Revisited: Input, Output and 'Throughput" (2012) 61(1) Political Studies 2. Papadopooulous and Warin also take a similar four strand approach in Y Papadopoulos & P Warin, 'Are Innovative, Participatory and Deliberative Procedures in Policy Making Democratic and Effective?'

(2007) 46 European Journal of Political Research 445.

43 For the use of similar criteria to assess direct democracy instruments see G Smith, Democratic Innovations - Designing Institutions for Citizen Participation (Cambridge University Press 2009).

44 J Schumpter, Capitalism, Socialism and Democracy (Allen and Unwin 1954).

45 Smith cites lack of impact and the heavy burden placed on citizens and institutions as two issues with direct democracy in Smith (n 38).

46 Schiller and Setala, for example, define popular initiatives as 'procedures that allow citizens to bring new issues to the political agenda ... through collecting a certain number of signatures in support of a policy proposal', in M Setala and T Schiller (eds), Citizens Initiatives in Europe: Procedures and Consequence of Agenda Setting by Citizens (Macmillan 2012) 1. Similarly Uleri in P Uleri 'Le forme di consultazione diretta. Uno Schema di classificazione per l'analisi comparata' (1981) 47 Rivista Italiana di Sciencia Politica described popular initiatives as "a procedure enabling a predetermined number of registered electors to submit a political demand", cited in V Cuesta Lopez, 'A Comparative Approach to the Regulation on the European Citizens Initiative' (2012) Perspectives on European Politics and Society 257, 258. For an outline of different forms of direct democracy instruments see B Kaufmann and J Pichler (eds) The European Citizens'Initiatives -- Into new democratic territory, (Intersentia 2010) 33-42.

47 M Setala and T Schiller (eds), Citizens Initiatives in Europe: Procedures and Consequence of Agenda Setting by Citizens (Macmillan 2012) 1 gives a detailed explanation of the distinction between full scale and agenda initiatives and discusses several examples of each from across Europe.

48 Full-scale initiatives are also called popular initiatives.

49 Some academics do not classify agenda-setting initiatives as direct democracy, eg, Smith (n 38).

50 South African Cases (Ethiopia v South Africa; Liberia v South Africa) [1966] ICJ Rep 6, at para 98.

51 For examples from across Europe see M Setala and T Schiller (eds), 'Citizens Ini-

tiatives in Europe: Procedures and Consequences of Agenda-setting by Citizens'
(Macmillan 2012).

52   See, for example, A Warleigh, 'On the Path to Legitimacy? The EU Citizens Initiative Right from a Critical Deliberativist Perspective', in C Ruzza and V Della Sala (eds), Governance and Civil Society in the European Union (Manchester University Press 2007) 55.

53   Quoted from speech by Vice President of the European Commission Maros Sefcovic, 'The Lisbon Treaty: Enhancing Democracy' on Sept 30th 2010, at 2. europa.eu/rapid/press-release_SPEECH-10-502_en.htm   europa.eu/rapid/press-release_SPEECH-10-502_en.htm.

54   J Organ, 'Decommissioning Direct Democracy? A critical analysis of Commission decision making on the legal admissibility of European Citizens Initiative proposals' (2014) 10(3) European Constitutional Law Review 422

55   C Berg & J Thompson (eds), An ECI that Works: Learning From the First Two Years of the ECI (2014). Available online: <http://www.citizens-initiative.eu/wp-content/uploads/2019/06/Berg_2014_Berg_Thomson_An_ECI_That_Works.pdf>

56   A Karatzia, 'The European Citizens Initiative and the EU Institutional Balance: On Realism and the Possibilities of Affecting EU Lawmaking' (2017) 54(1) Common Market Law Review 177.

57   See for instance, C Kissling, 'The Legal and Political Status of International Parliamentary Institutions' (Committee for a Democratic UN 2011)

58   R Blaug, 'Engineering Democracy' (2002) 50(1) Political Studies 102.

59   Art 11(4) TEU.

60   These important characteristics are defined more precisely in Regulation 211/2011, which implemented the ECI and is discussed further below.

61   For further comment on the type of democratic instrument that the ECI is defined as see A Auer, 'European Citizens Initiative' (2005) 1 European Constitutional Law Review 79. One point of disagreement is over the use of the term Popular Initiative, which Auer limits to instruments that 'grant the right to a

number of citizens to submit a draft constitutional or legislative provision to the voters, with no possibility of it being blocked by Parliament'. The authors of the present report would refer to these instruments as full-scale initiatives.

62 The phrase 'for the purpose of implementing the treaties' is taken by the Commission to mean that an ECI cannot make a proposal that requires treaty change.

63 For example it set the number of members states that are needed for a successful ECI.

64 "The procedure of an agenda initiative contains various steps and requirements. The main elements are admissible topics, the registration of the proposal and checking its legality, the quorum of required signatures, and the procedure of presentation and consideration in the state parliament." Schiller, in Setala and Schiller (eds) at 94.

65 Recital 8 Reg. 211/2011 and also in Amendment 23 justification European Parliament report.

66 Recital 8 Reg. 211/2011.

67 UNGA Res 1991 (XVIII) (17 December 1963) UN Doc A/RES/1991.

68 Organ (n 49).

69 Rule 38, UNGA Rules of Procedure.

70 M Hilf & D-E Khan, 'Article 22' in B Simma, The Charter of the United Nations: A Commentary (2nd edn, vol 1, Oxford University Press 2002) 420, 423.

71 See, importantly, D Sarooshi, 'The Legal Framework Governing United Nations Subsidiary Organs (1996) 67 British Institute of International Law 416.

72 P Szasz, 'The Complexification of the United Nations System' (1999) 3 Max Planck Yearbook of United Nations Law 3, 3.

73 Article 22' 429.

74 The first of these was Anagnostakis v European Commission Case C-589/15 P

75 See, UNSC Res 1904 (2009).

76 See, UNSC Res 2083 (2012) and 2161 (2014).

77 This is a change to the regulation about to be passed.

78 Schiller & Setala (n 41) 8.

79 UNGA Res 1991 (XVIII) (17 December 1963) UN Doc A/RES/1991.

80 Draft report on the proposal for a regulation of the European Parliament and of the Council on the citizens' initiative, Committee of Constitutional Affairs - COM(2010)0119 -- C7-0089/2010 -- 2010/0074(COD).

81 Ibid Amendment 33.

82 Ibid Amendment 61.

83 Claim based on the high percentage of people that abandon the online process to support ECIs.

84 Details of 'Right to Water ECI available at https://ec.europa.eu/citizens-initiative/public/initiatives/successful/details/2012/000003

85 T-561/14 - One of Us and Others v Commission - http://curia.europa.eu/juris/liste.jsf?language=en&num=T-561/14

86 MN Shaw, International Law (8th edn, Cambridge University Press 2017) 930.

87 Article 20 (UN Charter 1945).

88 Article 24, UN Charter (1945).

89 Article 25 and 103, UN Charter (1945).

90 Article 39, UN Charter (1945).

91 Art 31, UN Charter (1945) and Rule 37, Security Council Provisional Rules of Procedure.